PENTIMENTO

MICHAEL ALAN HERMAN

AMERICAN GRIFFIN
★

Pentimento

Published by American Griffin

ISBN: 978-0-9961211-2-5

this one is for the little monsters

the sad clowns

the sidewalk dreamers

and the ones that keep coming back

after you think they are gone

LETTER TO THE READER/ARTIST

So…as it turns out, not every painting is done on a clean white canvas. Sometimes an artist will take an existing work and paint right over the top of it, transforming portraits into landscapes and back again.

But it's not perfect. In the process, impressions from the previous painting can bleed through. We call these impressions – PENTIMENTO. Literally "repentance" in Italian, because the artist chose to change the piece.

I adore these hidden forms. These canvas ghosts. They can transform even the most ordinary picture into surrealism. A jazz singer can suddenly be one-part palace, a graveyard can be the portrait of a fisherman. To me, a pentimento is the best evidence that life is an act of collage and that art is not a finite expression, but an ever-evolving conversation that has been going on long before we got here and will continue far after we're gone.

And we get to contribute a verse.

With love,

Michael Alan Herman

THE DRIPPING BOOK

One time, I found a book in my room that drips ink.

Like something off Pinterest, it just expels

down the spine and onto the floor and into my mind.

Most nights, I can hear the ink when I'm trying to sleep

dripping like a heartbeat in the floorboards or a sink

and I don't think it's going to stop, so –

Last night, I spent a whole hour trying to shake it dry

like Pollock, or something more undone,

I grabbed the cover like fists and shook that book

back and forth

and up and down

over and over

rattling around

until there was ink all over the walls

and down my face

and across my arms

until my whole world smelt like paper has to.

And just like that,

the book stopped dripping.

For a few seconds

as I considered becoming a Business Major or something.

But then it continued to ooze

thick and velvet inky darkness as it had before

one tear at a time.

And it's been dripping ever since, so –

It's my favorite thing to brag about at parties.

KINTSUGI

When it is time to pull the lightbulb from out of my throat

and spread the pieces on the table.

When you arrange them first by shape and then by color,

let me be porcelain, cracks and all.

Even stained glass needs to be broken for colors.

We will not die as other things if we don't first

let the pieces

shatter.

You looked at me like I was the last thing in the world

and said,

in Japan they have an artform of mixing gold and cracks

taking what was mineral and pure

and letting it be a broken thing

because even gold deserves the chance to fade.

I can take these pieces of myself

make a wind chime, make a nest

it would be all the sounds inside my head

shrill, undefined, and even insecure

but distilled – distilled enough to mean something,

like the best poetry, broken wide open to be true.

NEVER HAVE I EVER

Have you ever

tried slicing yourself into ribbons of Courier New?

Stretched clean over canvas?

Oh, my dear,

look at us now, all carved up like patchwork

thin, like glass

and just as sharp.

Someone has to keep track of the way leaves change.

You asked me why it had to be like that

like there was a choice.

Oh, my sweet, darling, boy,

the color and clay in your fists,

the air in your throat, orange and alive,

you already know.

Because marble still makes you move.

Because there are so many colors in the shadows.

How could you have a choice

when there are veins in the Pietà?

A CASUAL OEUVRE

It takes

so much ink

to live.

ODE TO THE GHOST IN MY CLOSET

There is a ghost in my closet, and he looks just like me.

He stares with large bulbus eyes, reflecting like a child,
waiting for what I couldn't begin to guess.
I've tried calling out to him, pulling from my ribs,
Come here, little one. Come here.
And he hears me, but he does not move.
He just continues to wait and watch,
like some old Greek statue without arms.

Sometimes, we spend whole afternoons looking at each other
covered in the night before
just staring and wondering who will talk first,
but he never does, so I guess I lose that game.

Sometimes, I think I'm being too loud, I yell,
Why don't you make noise, break things, move, scare people?
But he doesn't like answering questions.
He just likes to watch, vacant and alone.

Sometimes, late at night,

when I've changed more than I thought I could,

I think he won't recognize me when I open the door again

but he is always there

waiting, like glass, or the shimmer on crayons

there are so many more mirrors in the world than we think.

There is a ghost in my closet, and he looks just like me.

DISCLAIMER PER DIEM

Art, even at its best, is labor.

No matter the medium.

No matter the message.

Your muse isn't gone,

He/she/they will return.

There is poetry even in the stillness,

I say to myself over and over again.

If repetition works for cults,

why not me?

COTTAGECORE LOVER

Sometimes

you smell more like evening air

than I think I can bear.

COLLARBONES

Thin and ribbed, always begging me to look underneath,

I can't edit myself when I am with you.

There is no ding at the end of the typeset to bring me back

the words just flow and burn like molten lead

and the ink spreads down your form and through my mind

like textures I want to know.

You, curled in the print of the bed, spread open like origami

with folds begging to be creased.

I thought I knew what seafoam tasted like before you,

but they don't give out disclaimers for living poetry,

they don't even warn you.

Instead, like my hands, I wander, trace, move

until I remember how badly I want to taste like you.

And always back to the bones,

the forms that define us.

I better not take a Rorschach test.

WHEN I LISTENED TO THE WAVES FOR TOO LONG

Please excuse me as I become violently introspective

the waves say to me as they spin around themselves

like Lavacourt under Snow.

Currents always seem to know just where to go

even if it's just to die on the shore.

CHILDGLOW ON THE DRIVER'S SIDE

I keep forgetting to tell you

brown eyes are the prettiest color,

anyone who disagrees clearly hasn't seen a sunset

rich, dark, velvet in the sky.

And that's not even talking about how they fleck

like something called goldstone I always see

in rock shops on vacation,

which is now my favorite rock,

because obsession is kind of the only way I exist,

not that I haven't tried other things,

but it also just makes for really good art,

so, this is my official reminder to tell you about brown eyes.

Sometime.

THE KITE FACTORY

I imagine

if you set us all up on display, the whole human race,

we would look like a collection of kites

dangling in the wind

flapping

free, but for a single cord

that keeps us from getting too far away.

We have to name that cord from time to time

my mother's eyes told me

warm and Irish like everything I aspire to be

in my childhood home

where I do my best monologuing.

We have to name that cord

because it's really the only thing that's required to be a kite.

And to fly.

Her fingers trace the scalp she's always held

and I know

even when the wind is gone, a kite is not a kite without a cord.

HELLO, MY NAME IS...

Stranger: What do you do?

Me: I battle the tyranny of the blank page.

Stranger:

Me:

Stranger:

Me:

Stranger:

Me:

Stranger:

Me: What do you do?

NAMES ARE THE BEST SOUNDS

Pretty girl in my bed, I want to make up a word for you.

With your pretty teeth, and your pretty smile,

it would be all the best parts of the words I know.

All the ooo's and oh's.

The r's and mmm's that come after that.

I would mix them together in a pot

blend them until they are more each other than themselves.

I would cool and cake with colors and clay

whisper them into a form with my lips

fashion these new sounds

until they have been every stage of matter.

Then, when my hands, my bones, are trembling,

I would press and kneed them, one after the other

faster and faster

until they form lines and arches, tissues,

whole letters that always should have been

faster and faster

until all my colors and ink and sounds and clay

are just a single

word.

Distilled, like you,

left to rest so it can be held,

because we are all moving around too much anyway.

I tell you, everyone would want to say it, bellow it out loud,

whisper it to the cool side of the pillow,

hold it soft and warm in the shallow of their palms,

but it would always be yours first.

Like a poem.

Or a name.

MY FORMAL ANSWER

A basin,

a pool,

a sea of ink

would not be enough.

              - Me to thee

NOW YOU KNOW

Doctor: What's your blood type?

Me: Take-Sumi, Fountain Black.

Doctor: Is that a type of ink?

Me:

Doctor:

Me:

Doctor:

Me:

Doctor:

Me: You got some or not?

CICERONE ON THE I-10

We are vessels of the big words we don't understand,

my mind said to itself over and over

as the highway, already burnt, stretched, I'm sure further

than it had before.

My face, a reflection of everything I held,

disjointed, and distant, until she spoke

spoke,

her old gray voice like silk,

We live in a polarized world.

She said into me.

All yes no, this that, hot cold,

but the antidote is to have a third thing

it keeps the balance right.

And I felt wisdom, crack along my skull,

like a dismissal from church,

spill through my lungs and around my edges

from a place, a face, that had lived, loved, and sat down

on her own porch steps with empathy.

Held hands like they were old southern belles

and had tea to spare.

Sat down on porch steps like there was new music playing

and there was a reason to play it.

Sat down and looked into each other's eyes

not to be seen, but to see.

And she looked at me,

through the cracks of the rearview mirror like a home,

like a guide you only meet once,

her eyes fresh water,

and I knew I had to write a poem.

THE SPACES BETWEEN LEAF STEMS

Promise me, right now, look up, and look for more colors.

Look for the shy ones

turquoise and liquorish green, rhubarb

and they will be there

lush and overflowing, more than before.

The impressionists knew it too,

they poured as many colors as they could into their drum

tight canvas, into the spaces between veins

the ridges of skin and bone.

Why can't there be red in the darkness?

Or orange in the sea?

It's always felt that way anyway.

Because they knew, like we all do,

the spaces between leaf stems are not so far away.

A MORALITY PLAY

We are

perhaps

unlike

in fabric

but we have

the same

seams.

IT'S TOO HARD TO STOP PAINTING WALLS

Sometimes, when I start painting walls

I don't know how to stop.

My palms, they move on their own, back and forth,

chasing color out of the room like flies

until I've known every edge of my indoor world

or at least the places I can reach.

I bend down, my spine heavy with Santa Fe Sunset

ready to exist in this new palette,

but I find myself already holding another brush,

spreading another surface, with another color,

over trim and chairs, lampshades and clothes,

right over mirrors

faster and faster

until my arms are wet and dotted

kaleidoscopic.

My eyes, mad like power,

I could change the whole world over

in the time it takes the chemicals to dry.

To the next house, and the next street, and the next

place I call a home.

Every window, and awning, and post,

nothing would be safe.

I could wash the whole world over and need another one

just to prove colors aren't meant to stay in cans.

Through crowds and over oceans, into the sky

right up until the moment I feel the scrape at the bottom

of the tin bin.

And I know the only way to continue is to buy more.

EFFIGY AS FUEL

If you peel back my skin, you won't find blood

only marble, dripping fresh like ink.

There is a hue inside us all that is deeper than tissue.

An acrylic something that mixes when we meet

and shake hands

and especially when we kiss.

The trick is to find colors that look good together

and not let them go

never let them go

because we need so many colors on the palette board

and both paint and blood are liquid.

A CASUAL CALL TO ARMS

Dear Future Self,

Promise me

you will always get up

to write it down.

ON VANITY

Dear Muse,

Please don't torch me.

- the polished shell

YOU KNOW WHERE

Oh, Fibonacci Girl, do you remember that place we found?

Where the walls, the air, the breath was thick and yellow?

Where they wrapped you full of syncopation

and let the rain fall all night?

I'd never heard music bubble like clay

vibrant as the masks I always have to wear.

Take me back to those sweet waters, high above the cement

ready to sweep her all away.

I told you dichotomy is my favorite salvation

but I should have known from the Feel Good Inc.

on the radio

a place can haunt you as much as a person.

ON EVERYDAY LIFE

I know

I am a protagonist,

but I don't know what genre this is yet.

PALETTE KNIFE

I scoop up a handful of the night

I hold her close to my heart

I tell her, *It's us against all of them now.*

CARPE NOCTEM

Slowly, like an afternoon, my chin somewhere on your neck

the space between us is always growing thinner.

I read somewhere,

in a romantic book, there is an alchemy to human souls,

how they collide and blend,

like colors you didn't expect to find.

If I could look down at that palette now

see the colors yet to come,

I would only want to go faster

press harder

deeper

into the places we both are

like two statues, hung upside down,

suspended and scraping against each other

faster and faster

until we are nothing but the dust in our lungs

and the folds in the clothes on the floor,

the exhibitions we make.

I think there is a reason veins look like hands.

THEY SELL WHITE CALACATTA AT STORES NOW

Everywhere I go, there are marble statues that follow me.

Their toes, like teeth, always clattering on the floor.

We make so many footprints on beaches,

and in terminals, and funeral homes,

really anywhere they can fit.

Some of them are missing limbs

or have cracks down their sides

but none of them have eyes.

I have to guess what they are thinking,

hungry and alive, as we move from place to place.

I don't think anyone else can see them

but I've never really asked, so –

We just keep marching up and down, like ghosts, or soldiers

or something more haunted, burnt down to a single word.

Some nights,

when I wake up and see them all standing around me

their eyes like dark water, I think they are versions of myself old versions that only my high school friends remember.

But I don't think I've been so many shapes

or even that many places,

scraped into bust after bust after bust

all the dust it must take to live.

It's impossible to tell who is reflecting who

when the lights are always this dim,

but I know they are going to be here for a while, so –

I have to get used to the sounds we make.

Writers are a whole bunch of people pretending to be one.

A GUST OF WIND PRETENDING TO BE A SONNET

Oh, let me be the wind, you be the fire.

With every gust let me be as the fuel

To play the jest of circular desire

And we'll make radiance to dull a yule.

For when I am alone in evening brine

A frozen fix of nerving anxious heat

I turn my breath back to our singular design

That each day more is now one less to beat.

My love, my muse, my single masterpiece

For you my breath, my beating heart, my youth.

For even now I feel your flames to feast

They grow and swell in me this single truth:

That I am lost, am found, all but desire

We are the heat in wind, the breath in fire.

RESTING MIDWESTERN FACE

I'm sorry, it's just my resting Midwestern face

my heart says to you as you walk into my life.

Sometimes I try to be too polite to exist.

ALL THE STUFF IN MY HEAD NEEDS STACKABLE DRAWERS

There are

so many things

in my room.

Forks and spoons bent into rings

shells and ribbons and bells

rows of books or records I don't remember buying

videotapes stretched off their frame

keys with wings

pointed things

and so many out of date, out of place shoes.

I might just tape them all to the wall.

If I could find the time to find the floor.

But I drive eighty-five on country roads

trying to break open my heart

or at least my mind

because a priest once told me my eyes

capture the world at 60 frames per second

and that's still not enough space to hold all the stuff I want

so —

I wring my hands

and stand in lines

and keep buying things for my carpet floor

already bowed so low it's going to crack.

There are

so many things

in my room.

And I wish I was talking about my room.

MY FAVORITE GHOST

Me:

Nostalgia:

Me:

Nostalgia:

Me:

Nostalgia:

Me:

Nostalgia:

Me: Haunt me.

ON THE EDGE OF REALITY AND LIGHT

What a piece of work is the <u>blank page</u>

How noble in reason, how infinite in faculty

In form and moving how express and admirable

In action how like a demon

In apprehension how like a tyrant.

I think to myself as I don't write

up and down the page until it is filled.

Thank God Hamlet is in the public domain.

EXPO DRY ERASE MARKER IN MY THROAT

There is an Expo Dry Erase Marker in my throat.

Thin and rodded, jet black, and mine,

I know it's there because I took it out and placed it

on the floor.

Full disclosure

I didn't mean to take it out, but I wasn't sure what it was,

and I wanted to make sure I didn't have a tumor or something,

but it's just an Expo Dry Erase Marker in my throat.

Oh yeah, and I tried writing with it

but it seems like it's out of ink.

The warning on the side said not to use it on cloth

or to shake it,

but I've tried both of those things now.

And it's not like

I need an Expo Dry Erase Marker in my throat,

at least not at this moment,

but I just like having the option to use one.

And I called to see if I could buy more ink

but they said I should just buy another marker.

And…I don't think they've ever had…

an Expo Dry Erase Marker in their throat

Because if they did, they would never have suggested

I just buy a new one like there were packs of them hanging

in stores, bundled together.

That said…

I read online if you leave it capped for 24 hours

usually the ink comes back.

So, I'm trying that, and I'll let you know how it goes.

IMPETUS

Because

some souls mix

when they meet.

WRITER'S BLOCK ON THE FRONT STEPS AGAIN

You haggard old bastard you.

You twisted old weed.

All hiss hiss and blow low.

I know we talked last time you were here,

I screamed my penance into your skull,

told you water was supposed to flow down river

gravity says so,

but I smelt your grin, sinning, thinning, spinning,

heard your hearse reeving from a mile away.

I knew you would be dropping by to casually strip my spine

like corn,

coming in here with that liquorish lip and rattlesnake soul

to twist the pieces of my back like pegs.

You look like a little bitch that gets away with it.

And I know you do, but not today.

Today, you're an echo, a chord.

And I'm already five senses up on the rest of you,

so, what's you're move, little man?

I've got royalty free music on my phone.

FIRST DAY

Stranger: What do you do?

Me: I turn blood into ink.

Stranger:

Me:

Stranger:

Me:

Stranger:

Me:

Stranger:

Me: What do you do?

WHEN MY WIFE WORE RIPPED JEANS ON SUNDAY

I like ripped jeans

they tell me where my fingers should go.

CONSTRUCTIVE CRITICISM

Hang on a minute.

I write you poems

you kiss me?

More ink,

more ink,

more.

AUBADE IN BLUE

Stretch the paper thin like canvas

pour your thoughts of ink like paint.

Write each word and precious detail

like it's love and unrestraint.

TOO MUCH WISDOM FOR THE SIXTH GRADE

The English teacher that changed my life once said:

You still haven't met all the people who will love you,

and I think that is still echoing in my skull.

SILVER LINING FARM

When my father told me to *go out and mine that silver lining*,

he didn't tell me what it would taste like.

No, he didn't say it would be like soap

thick and aphoristic

down the back of my throat

through my form

the heavy liquid hotter than I expected,

and all the time, back to you.

And the color of that rug.

The horn-tooth hook of the dining room table.

To a place, a home, a hollow, I didn't remember I had.

If you asked me, I would stay there,

full of night and crayons,

clinging, just clinging, with these harpooned hands

because we all still want the dinosaurs to be real

and the taillights to be something else

with scraped knees

and bees

and chalk.

So, I will hold these children's hands against the sun

like my father taught me, make a fortress for my eyes

because the clouds can get so thin sometimes

but they aren't gone yet.

No, they aren't gone yet.

I COULD FILL UP THE WHOLE PAGE BUT YOU GET THE IDEA

Insanity is doing the same thing, expecting a different result.

Finish your art.

Insanity is doing the same thing, expecting a different result.

Finish your art.

Insanity is doing the same thing, expecting a different result.

Finish your art.

Insanity is doing the same thing, expecting a different result.

Finish your art.

PREDESTINATION

Go to where time goes backwards for you

then start to write.

CLUTTERCORE HEART

I met a girl who grows flowers from her hands

and roses from her eyes.

Each fingerprint a petal, with stems and thorns like vines

so tight they could have been a fist.

I never knew I would be a botanist

I told her one day, walking down the furthest part of my mind

I'm getting into cluttercore, she said,

not as a choice, but as a framing device.

Sometimes the movies are just right

and sometimes they aren't

when you kneel in grass on your side

wearing khaki pants, you cleaned the week before.

Or when you dig into the clayed caked earth to hide

a secret or a seed, whichever can grow first.

I held her hand to feel the flora and fauna of her form

nothing else

the gentle pistils always tangling with mine.

I asked her to play make believe forever.

And she said yes.

DARK ACADEMIA

Oh, take me to a room with stained glass hearts

where tongues move, velvet and sideways

and there are just too many chandeliers.

Smiling is just showing our skulls to each other,

but you already knew that

because you have Horace Walpole tucked under your arm

and a raven in your heart.

I could live in those halls of your chest

memorize every stone and arch

until I was as beautiful as them.

They always keep secrets in the most beautiful places,

where the wonder bottoms out your chest.

Sweet, dark academia.

again,

again,

again.

WE ARE ALL JUST SANDCASTLES

When it comes down to it

rattling and shaking

next to that beautiful woman we call the sea

all blue and trimmed in white lace waves

like a proper Victorian,

we're all just lined up

some Greco-Roman, or Venetian, and me definitely Baroque,

but all of us sand.

Pasted together one pebble at a time.

But somehow, we still fight about what columns look like

and what buttresses are anyway

all night, and all day,

until our chests are buzzing like knives

scraped and wrapped like tongues,

it's the same small feet that bring us down

as the lampshades come on, so –

maybe we just listen to the sea,

the echo of so many waves come before,

and stand.

Like castles.

TO THAT YOUTUBE CHANNEL THAT TALKS ABOUT WHY FILMS SUCK

I saw the other day

that picture frames are growing

in my next-door neighbor's yard

right out of the ground

like you'd think they belonged there.

And that's great, but now

no one can walk down the block without being on display,

cropped into something or somewhere or someway,

and that's fine if you're made of plastic

but I'm not, I'm paper at best.

I tell you what, if all the world's a stage

there isn't that much space for an audience.

And certainly not that many pixels, so –

No. No snide comments like hedge funds.

No drilling into skulls.

I swear,

and you can dissect the extended universe of this statement, if you started writing

the spaces in your teeth wouldn't be so big.

How does it feel

to be the physical personification of white noise?

A BAD DAY IS THE MOST UNHELPFUL ROOMBA

I don't have much more to say

except

some days are built that way.

And some Roombas.

MY CAPRICE

You can have everything in life, just not all at the same time,
the grandfather clock says to me again and again
every fifteen minutes if I'm lucky.
The longer you know a thing, the more you personify it.

CLINICAL BUT TRUE

Absence makes the art grow stronger.

Absence makes the art grow stronger.

Absence makes the art grow stronger.

WHERE THE IMAGES GO

Last month it was glass and how it shatters,

this month it's chasms.

You know how you get obsessed with certain images

and then refuse to let them go?

Like a song you have to play until you hate

If I could have a map

a rolodex of those images printed as big as they can on a wall

I want to know where those patterns would go.

Do you think there would be a theme?

One color palette that emerges from the rest?

I know this is more philosophy than poetry,

but I like to play Pictionary with myself

painting the same square over and over

retracing my steps until they inescapably come back to you.

And your color palette.

And theme.

And images.

The new forms they make when we overlap.

Where do those images go?

DEAREST TYRANNY OF THE BLANK PAGE

Sometimes, I spend whole afternoons sat down on rocks

staring at the voidless, endless chasm in my chest.

I have felt the wallpaper of this rapture, dusty and cracked,

between my fingers so many times.

The expectation of being a god

is something no one should have to live up too.

So, I breathe, slowly into that space,

that ocean of empty blank white dressed up in potential,

hoping, praying even heavy air could fill it, or kill it

whichever came first.

They said, you can go anywhere you want,

the world is your oyster,

dream it and be it,

but I spend so much time staring at screens, ultra-bright white

so I can illuminate the places inside myself I am afraid to see.

There's a reason those screens are black mirrors

and the cursor is always flashing

and the battery is slowly dying

and the minutes are on their own agenda

spinning like tops no one wound up

and just as my flesh is about to eat itself alive

my heart screams, loud enough, even for my mind

there is poetry in the stillness, in the silence.

There's a muse there too, wrapped full in deep purple

listen to her and she'll whisper

just for you

right into your skull

It's not too late. It's never too late.

MY SINGLE WISH

I hope

you and your inklings

are on parade tonight.

THE MANIFESTO OF THE BROKEN HEARTED

The manifesto of the broken hearted comes in business casual,

in lines of A4 paper, in rows where time doesn't exist

at least, that's how they've always done it,

like casinos, pumping more air into the room so time

stretches to 5:05, to the next week, to the next month

all the way to empty hands, broken open like shells.

Promise me, when you are there,

you will always remember that deep pyre,

those coals,

it takes life force to bring forms out of marble

to give them flesh

all the greats have said so.

So, not yet.

Hear these words, not yet.

One more piece of paper.

One more layer of ink.

Because this truth is, and always will be, greater than theirs:

You never know

which one of your creations

will become someone's favorite.

The one they will need, the one they will never put down

long after they have looked away, so –

keep going, little one, keep going.

Breath in, then out, to fan the flames

and show us that pyre.

Right this moment if you can.

Thank you, my childglow.

Here's to many more.

And many more.